The United States

Kansas

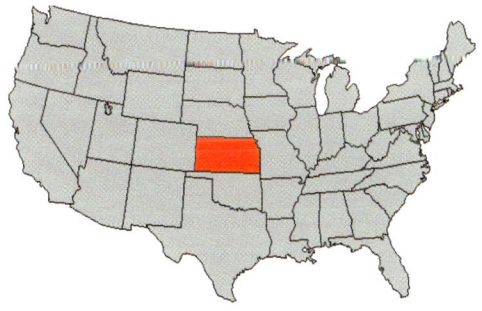

Anne Welsbacher
ABDO & Daughters

visit us at
www.abdopub.com

Published by Abdo & Daughters, 4940 Viking Drive, Suite 622, Edina, Minnesota 55435. Copyright © 1998 by Abdo Consulting Group, Inc., Pentagon Tower, P.O. Box 36036, Minneapolis, Minnesota 55435 USA. International copyrights reserved in all countries. No part of this book may be reproduced in any form without written permission from the publisher.

Printed in the United States.

Cover and Interior Photo credits: Peter Arnold, Inc., Super Stock, Archive Photos

Edited by Lori Kinstad Pupeza
Contributing editor Brooke Henderson
Special thanks to our Checkerboard Kids—Tyler Wagner, Annie O'Leary, Morgan Roberts, Kenny Abdo

All statistics taken from the 1990 census; The Rand McNally Discovery Atlas of The United States. Other sources: *Kansas*, Fradin and Fradin, Children's Press, Chicago, 1997; *Kansas*, Kent, Children's Press, Chicago, 1991; *Kansas*, Fredeen, Lerner Publications Co., Minneapolis, 1992; America Online, Compton's Living Encyclopedia, 1997; World Book Encyclopedia, 1990.

Library of Congress Cataloging-in-Publication Data

Welsbacher, Anne, 1955-
    Kansas / Anne Welsbacher.
    p.   cm. -- (United States)
    Includes index.
    Summary: Presents information about the history, geography, and people of the midwestern state known as the "Sunflower State."
    ISBN 1-56239-879-2
    1. Kansas--Juvenile literature. [1. Kansas.] I. Title. II. Series: United States (Series)
    F681.3.W45   1998
    978.1--dc21
                                                     97-23776
                                                      CIP
                                                      AC

Contents

Welcome to Kansas 4
Fast Facts About Kansas 6
Nature's Treasures 8
Beginnings 10
Happenings 12
Kansas's People 18
Kansas's Cities 20
Kansas's Land 22
Kansas at Play 24
Kansas at Work 26
Fun Facts 28
Glossary 30
Internet Sites 31
Index 32

Welcome to Kansas

Kansas was a part of the wild west. Cowboys and outlaws roamed its countryside. Today, wheat fields and airplane factories cover a lot of Kansas.

Kansas is in the very middle of the United States mainland! For this reason, it is sometimes called Midway, U.S.A.

Kansas grows more wheat than all but one state. Wheat is used to make bread. So Kansas also is called the Breadbasket of America.

Sunflowers grow all over the prairies of Kansas. The best known nickname for Kansas is the Sunflower State.

Opposite page: Kansas is known as the sunflower state.

Fast Facts

KANSAS
Capital
Topeka (119,883 people)
Area
81,783 square miles
(211,817 sq km)
Population
2,485,600 people
Rank: 32nd
Statehood
January 29, 1861
(34th state admitted)
Principal rivers
Arkansas River
Kansas River
Highest point
Mount Sunflower;
4,039 feet (1,231 m)
Largest city
Wichita (304,011 people)
Motto
Ad astra per aspera
(To the stars through difficulties)
Song
"Home on the Range"
Famous People
Thomas Hart Benton, Amelia Earhart, Dwight D. Eisenhower, Carry Nation, William Allen White

State Flag

Western Meadowlark

Sunflower

Cottonwood

About Kansas
The Sunflower State

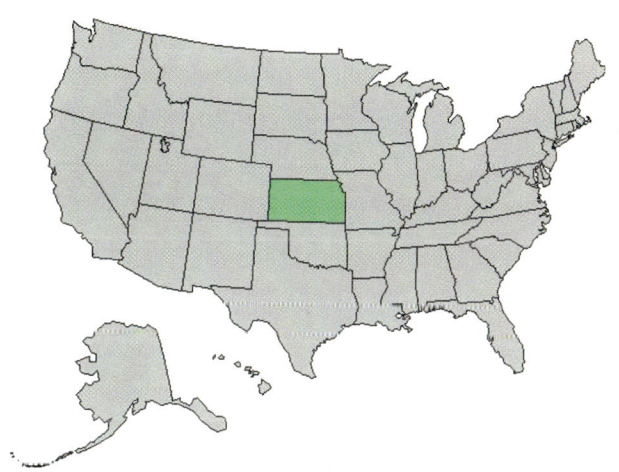

Detail area

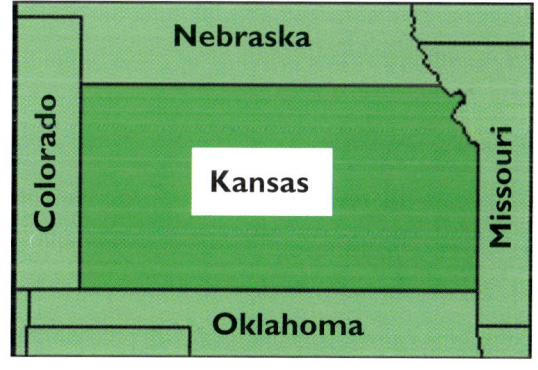

Kansas's abbreviation

Borders: west (Colorado), north (Nebraska), east (Missouri), south (Oklahoma)

Nature's Treasures

Most of Kansas has rich soil. It is good for farming. In the southwest part of the state, the land is sandy. There are even sand dunes.

In the 1930s and 1950s, there were **droughts**. Because there wasn't any rain, the dry soil blew away. People couldn't grow corn, wheat, or other crops because there wasn't enough water.

Kansans learned to **conserve** water. Kansas does not have many lakes. So Kansans built them.

They also grew grass. This helped keep the soil in place. There is still grass throughout the state.

Kansas has many minerals like oil and gas. It also has clay, coal, helium, salt, gravel, and stone.

An oil well in a Kansas wheat field.

Beginnings

Native Americans first came to Kansas about 10,000 years ago. Among them were the Kaw, or **Kansa**, people. Their name means "people of the south wind." Osage, Pawnee, and Wichita were other Native Americans who lived in Kansas.

In the 1600s and 1700s, fur trappers and settlers came to Kansas from France. In 1803, France sold Kansas and other areas to the United States.

In the 1800s, **immigrants** moved to the United States. They pushed Native Americans further west, many into Kansas. Later, they were forced to go even further south and west.

In the mid-1800s, southern states had slavery. Northern states did not. The Civil War was started over whether or not new states should allow slavery.

In Kansas, many people fought and died over slavery. This time period was named **Bleeding Kansas**. The people who did not want slavery were called **abolitionists**. Those who did want it were called **pro-slavers**.

Finally, Kansas decided it would not have slavery. It became the 34th state in 1861.

In the late 1800s, **pioneers** traveled west through Kansas. The pioneers rode in covered wagons.

Cowboys drove cattle across Kansas. "Cow" towns like Dodge City were born. They had outlaws and shoot-outs with sheriffs.

Today, Kansas has more highways than most states. Many airplanes are made in Kansas. So today, people travel through Kansas in cars and planes instead of covered wagons!

Cowboys driving cattle.

Happenings • Happenings • Happenings • Happenings • Happenings • Happenings

1000 to 1821

The First Kansans

 1000-1500s: Kaw, Osage, Pawnee, and Wichita people farm the Kansas land.

 1700s: French fur trappers and settlers move into Kansas. Tribes are pushed further west from the eastern United States.

 1821: The Santa Fe Trail opens. Many people begin crossing the United States. They travel through Kansas.

appenings • Happenings • Happenings • Happenings • Happenings • Happenings

Kansas
1000 to 1821

Happenings • Happenings • Happenings • Happenings • Happenings • Happenings

1854 to 1861

Troubled Times

 1854: The Kansas-Nebraska Act is passed. The law says Kansas must decide whether to have slaves or not.

 1854-1858: **Abolitionists** and **pro-slavers** fight in **Bleeding Kansas**.

 1860: The Pony Express begins carrying mail across Kansas.

 1861: Kansas becomes the 34th state. The Civil War begins.

appenings • Happenings • Happenings • Happenings • Happenings • Happenings

Kansas
1854 to 1861

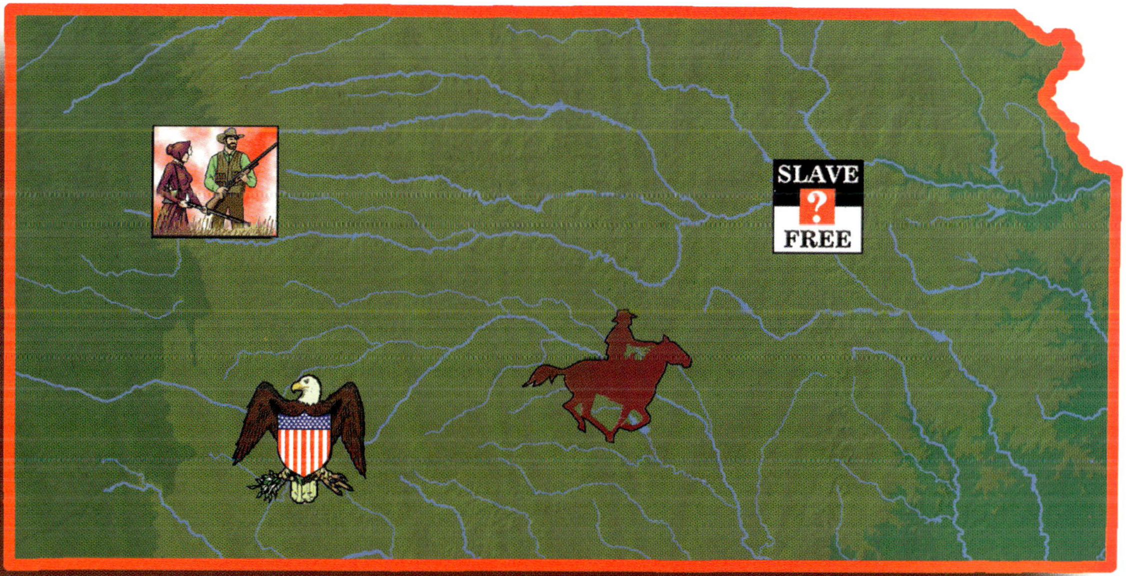

15

Happenings • Happenings • Happenings • Happenings • Happenings • Happenings

1925 to Today

Modern Times

 1925: The famous Menninger clinic for the mentally ill opens in Topeka.

 1930s: **Droughts** bring dust storms. Many farmers suffer.

 1954: A Law is passed that makes it illegal to keep whites and African Americans separate in schools.

 1956: The Kansas Turnpike is built.

appenings • Happenings • Happenings • Happenings • Happenings • Happenings

Kansas
1925 to Today

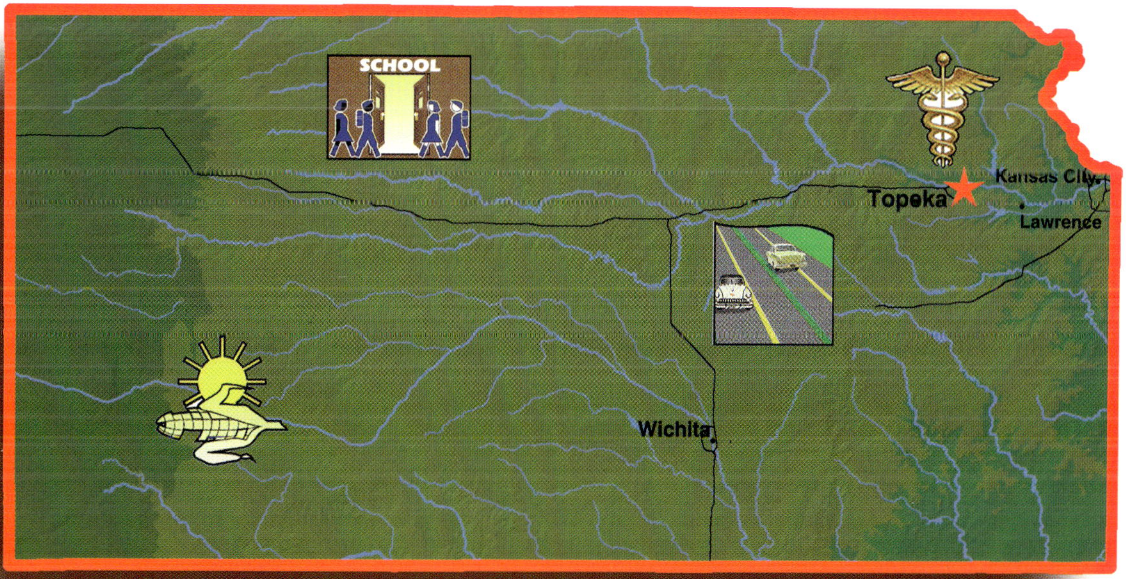

Kansas's People

There are about 2.5 million people in Kansas. Many live in cities. Some live in **rural** areas.

The poet and author of children's books, Gwendolyn Brooks, was born in Topeka. Other Kansas writers were William Allen White, William Inge, and Damon Runyon.

Hugh Beaumont was from Lawrence, Kansas. He played Beaver's father in the TV show, "Leave it to Beaver." Dennis Hopper, who was in the movie *Hoosiers*, is from Dodge City. And silent movie star Buster Keaton was from Piqua.

Hattie McDaniel was from Wichita. She was the first African American to win an Academy Award. She played Mammy in *Gone with the Wind*. Kirstie Alley, from the TV show "Cheers," was also born in Wichita. Vivian Vance, who played Ethel Mertz on the TV show "I Love Lucy," was from Cherryvale, Kansas.

Amelia Earhart, the first woman to attempt to fly across the Atlantic Ocean, was from Atchison. Olympic winner Jim Ryun was the first high school student to run a mile in less than four minutes. He was from Wichita. And many political leaders were born in Kansas. They include Senators Nancy Kassebaum and Bob Dole, who was the 1996 Republican Presidential candidate.

Gwendolyn Brooks

Amelia Earhart

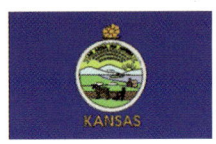

Kansas's Cities

The largest city in Kansas is Wichita. It is along the Arkansas River. It is called the Air Capital of the World because so many airplanes are built there.

The next largest city is Kansas City. Next to it is Overland Park. The capital of Kansas is Topeka. It is the third largest city in Kansas.

Other cities are Lawrence, Manhattan, and Hutchinson. Smith Center is a very small town, but it is famous. Near it is the exact middle of the mainland United States!

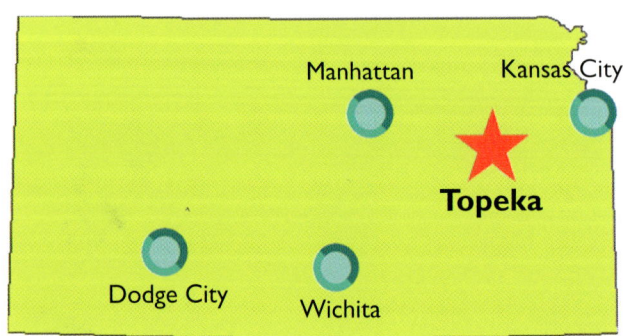

A view of downtown Topeka, Kansas

Kansas's Land

Kansas is shaped like a box with a broken corner. That corner, in the northeast part of the state, has hills and high bluffs. On the western side are the Great Plains. Here Kansas is mostly flat.

Eastern Kansas has low hills. The Flint Hills are made of limestone. A pretty, long grass called bluegrass or **bluestem** grows on the Flint Hills.

The Arkansas River runs from western to south-central Kansas. Then it flows into Oklahoma and Arkansas. In Kansas the Arkansas River is called the "ar-KAN-sus." But in Arkansas, it is called the "AR-kan-saw," like the state!

There are almost 200 kinds of grasses in Kansas! Tall bluestems are in the east. In the west are buffalo grass and tumbleweeds. Sunflowers grow all through Kansas. Asters, clover, thistles, and morning-glories are other wild flowers in Kansas.

Once there were many buffalo in Kansas. Hunters, however, killed almost all of them. Today there aren't as many buffalo roaming the countryside. Other animals in Kansas are coyotes, opossums, and rabbits.

Hawks, woodpeckers, crows, and blue jays fly the Kansas skies. Catfish swim in its lakes. And rattlesnakes slither through its grasses.

Kansas is cold in the winter and hot in the summer. In the spring it has tornadoes. Dorothy flew to Oz in a Kansas tornado!

Flint Hills, Morris County, Kansas.

Kansas at Play

Cowtown, in Wichita, has buildings and streets that look just like they did in the wild west days. Native American and western artists put their art in the Wichita Art Museum.

More than two million bugs are on display at a museum in Lawrence! In Hutchinson, the Kansas Cosmosphere and Space Center has the world's largest collection of space suits.

The Hutchinson State Fair is held every September. Other yearly events are the summer River Festival in Wichita, the June Flint Hills Rodeo, and the fall Bluegrass Festival in Winfield, Kansas.

Opposite page: Two young cowboys in Kansas.

Kansas at Work

Many Kansans grow wheat. Millions of tons of wheat are grown in Kansas. Farmers also grow corn and raise cows for beef.

Most of the small airplanes made in the United States are made in Kansas. Kansans also make helicopters, train cars, train engines, and snowplows.

Some Kansans work at the army base or the prison in Leavenworth, Kansas. Others work at one of the **colleges** in Wichita, Lawrence, Manhattan, or other towns.

Many Kansans work in service. They work in banks, places to eat, and hospitals. They also sell beef, airplanes, and other things that are made in Kansas.

Opposite page: Many people in Kansas work in airplane factories.

Fun Facts

- The first woman mayor in the United States was Susanna Salter, mayor of Argonia, Kansas, in 1887.
- The first Native American newspaper in North America was printed in Kansas in 1835. The Siwinowe Kesibwi (Shawnee Sun) was written in the language Algonquian.
- The largest **meteorite** in the world landed in Kansas 2,000 years ago. It weighed 2,240 pounds (1,016 kilograms).
- Kansas has more miles of highway than most other states. The exact middle of the mainland United States is near Smith Center, Kansas.
- President Abraham Lincoln once said, "If I went west, I think I would go to Kansas."
- The original Pony Express is in Marysville, Kansas. It began as a way to send mail in the 1850s. People on horseback would carry mail across the country.

The Pony Express homestation #1 in Marshall County, Kansas, still stands as a memorial.

The Pony Express in 1859.

Glossary

Abolitionist: a person who did not want slavery during the time before the Civil War.

Bleeding Kansas: the period of time, from 1855 to 1861, when many people in the Kansas area fought over whether or not to have slavery.

Bluestem: a tall grass that grows in eastern Kansas.

College: a school you can go to after finishing high school.

Conserve: to save, to not use any more than you need.

Drought: a long period of time with no rain or snow.

Immigrant: a person who comes from another country.

Kansa: early people of Kansas; the name means "people of the south wind."

Latino: a person whose family came from Central America or South America.

Meteorite: a rock from outer space.

Pioneer: a person who goes somewhere for the first time.

Pro-slaver: a person who did want slavery during the time before the Civil War.

Rural: country, with no big cities close by.

Internet Sites

Kansas Community Networks
http://history.cc.ukans.edu/heritage/towns
A bunch of community networks in Kansas and historial information about Kansas towns.

Kansas Children's Network
http://www.state.ks.us/public/kidsnet
A service to the children of Kansas, their parents, and others who work with them.

These sites are subject to change. Go to your favorite search engine and type in Kansas for more sites.

PASS IT ON

Tell Others Something Special About Your State

To educate readers around the country, pass on interesting tips, places to see, history, and little unknown facts about the state you live in. We want to hear from you!

To get posted on ABDO & Daughters website E-mail us at "mystate@abdopub.com"

Index

A

abolitionist 11, 14
African Americans 16
airplane factories 4
animals 23
Arkansas River 6, 20, 22
artists 24

B

Bleeding Kansas 11, 14
bluestem 11
Brooks, Gwendolyn 18
buffalo 22, 23

C

cities 18, 20, 28
Civil War 10, 14
colleges 26
covered wagons 11
cowboys 4, 11

D

Dodge City 11, 18
drought 8, 16

E

Earhart, Amelia 6, 19

F

farming 8
France 10
fur trappers 10, 12

G

Great Plains 22

I

immigrants 10

K

Kansa 4, 10
Kansas Cosmosphere and Space Center 24
Kansas Turnpike 16
Kansas-Nebraska Act 14

L

lakes 8, 23

M

meteorite 28
Midway, U.S.A. 4
minerals 8

N

Native Americans 10

P

pioneers 11
Pony Express 14
prairies 4
pro-slaver 11, 14

R

river 6, 22, 24
rural areas 18

S

Santa Fe Trail 12
settlers 10, 12
slavery 10
soil 8
sunflowers 4, 22

T

Topeka 6, 16, 18, 20
tornadoes 23

W

wheat 4, 8, 26
Wichita 6, 10, 12, 18, 20, 24, 26
Wichita Art Museum 24
wild west 4, 24